Gymnastics

BY M. K. OSBORNE

D1296787

AMICUS | AMICUS INK

Amicus High Interest is published by Amicus and Amicus Ink
P.O. Box 1329, Mankato, MN 56002
www.amicuspublishing.us

Library of Congress Cataloging-in-Publication Data
Names: Osborne, M. K., author.
Title: Gymnastics / by M.K. Osborne.
Description: Mankato, Minnesota : Amicus/Amicus Ink, [2020]
 | Series: Summer olympic sports | Audience: Grades: K to
 grade 3. | Includes bibliographical references and index.
Identifiers: LCCN 2019001946 (print) | LCCN 2019013374
 (ebook) | ISBN 9781681518633 (pdf) |
 ISBN 9781681518237 (library binding) |
 ISBN 9781681525518 (pbk.)
Subjects: LCSH: Gymnastics–Juvenile literature. | Olympics–
Juvenile literature.
Classification: LCC GV461.3 (ebook) | LCC GV461.3 .O74
 2020 (print) | DDC 796.44–dc23
LC record available at https://lccn.loc.gov/2019001946

Editor: Wendy Dieker
Designer: Aubrey Harper
Photo Researcher: Shane Freed

Photo Credits: Melissa J. Perenson/Cal Sport Media/AP cover;
DAMIR SAGOLJ/REUTERS/Newscom 4; Popperfoto/Getty 7;
ABC Photo Archives/Getty 8; PCN Black/Alamy 10–11, 15;
Gregory Bull/AP 12; Alan Edwards/Alamy 16; ZUMA Press/
Alamy 18–19; Nippon News/Alamy 20, 24; Mike Blake/
Newscom 23; Julie Jacobson/AP 27; Ben Stansall/Getty 28

Printed in the United States of America

HC 10 9 8 7 6 5 4 3 2 1
PB 10 9 8 7 6 5 4 3 2 1

Table of Contents

Gold medalist Aliya Mustafina
of Russia makes difficult skills
look easy.

Going for the Gold

Every four years, we watch the world's best athletes meet at the Summer Olympic Games. What's one of the most popular events to watch? Gymnastics. These events highlight athletes with strength and grace. Poise, control, and personality are what wow the judges. Who will win the gymnastics gold medals?

Gymnastics was featured at the first Olympic Games in 1896. At that time, only men competed. They competed in rope climbing and club swinging—which was sort of like juggling. But they also did events we see today. They flipped over the vault. They swung around on the parallel and horizontal bars. They showed upper body strength on the rings.

A Norwegian gymnast competes on the high bar in the 1912 Olympics.

Mary Lou Retton inspired many girls to be gymnasts after she won a gold medal in 1984.

 Did women have Olympic gymnastics events before 1952?

Women started competing in individual Olympic events in 1952. Soon after, they became celebrity athletes. Nadia Comaneci stunned fans with perfect routines in 1976. In 1984, U.S. fans watched Mary Lou Retton become the first U.S. gymnast to win an individual medal. Today, gymnastics is one of the most-watched events of the Summer Games.

 Yes. Women had team gymnastics events in 1928, 1936, and 1948.

Artistic Gymnastics

The most famous gymnasts are artistic gymnasts. These gymnasts do a routine on an **apparatus**, or piece of equipment. Judges score them on how well they do a routine. But they also get scored on the moves they do. Harder moves get higher scores. Both men and women compete in artistic events.

U.S. gymnast Jacob Dalton shows strength on the rings.

Judges on both sides of the beam watch each gymnast's routine carefully.

Q What is the highest score a gymnast can get?

Two panels of judges watch each routine. One group adds up **difficulty points** for the moves the gymnast does. The other group watches that the moves are done well. A gymnast starts with ten **execution points**. Mistakes mean judges take points away. The two scores are added up for a final score.

 There is no maximum score. Most top gymnasts score 14s or 15s in their events. A few earn 16s.

Women compete in four different artistic events. Each event is designed to show different skills. The vault table features speed and agility. In the floor exercise, women show grace and tumbling skills. On the balance beam, poise and stamina earn points. Spins and flips around the uneven bars show fluid movements.

U.S. gold medalist Simone Biles twists in the air as she launches over the vault table.

Gold medalist Kohei Uchimura from Japan competes on the high bar.

Q Is the men's floor routine the same as the women's?

Men have six artistic events. Men's events focus on strength and agility. Men still compete in the same five individual events as they did in 1896. You will see vault, rings, and pommel horse. They also compete on the horizontal bar and parallel bars. But today, men also do a floor routine.

 Not really. Women's routines have music and are like a dance. Men's routines do not have music and focus on tumbling.

At the Olympics, both men and women compete in a **qualifying round**. The best gymnasts go on to the individual event finals. After that, the ones who do the best in the individual events also do the **all-around event**. These gymnasts do each event once more. Some gymnasts are very busy!

Madison Kocian competed on uneven bars three times at the 2016 Olympics.

The men's gymnastics team from Japan won the 2016 team gold medal.

 Which countries have the best teams?

Artistic gymnastics also includes a team event. The top 12 teams in the world compete at the qualifying round. Each team has four or five people. Only eight teams move on to the finals. In the finals, the team chooses three gymnasts to perform in each event. The scores are added up. The team with the highest score wins.

 For men, China and Japan almost always win team medals. For women, the United States and Romania have dominated.

Rhythmic Gymnastics

A rhythmic gymnast is part dancer, part acrobat. These women do routines with four different **props**. They spin hoops and twirl ribbons. They toss balls and clubs. All the while, they are doing handstands, spins, splits, and leaps. Gymnasts do one routine for each prop. The scores are added up. The gymnast with the highest total score wins the gold medal.

Yana Kudryavtseva of Russia
uses a hoop in her routine.

Colorful ribbons swirl as the group from Russia performs a rhythmic routine.

 What year did rhythmic gymnastics first appear at the Olympics?

One rhythmic gymnast is fun to watch. But a group of five women is truly amazing! Each group performs twice. The first routine features the ribbon. A second routine is a flurry of hoops and clubs. The team with the highest total score are the champions.

 The individual events were first featured in 1984. The group event was added in 1996.

Trampoline

On the other side of the gymnastics arena, a gymnast is bouncing on a trampoline. Since 2000, fans have been thrilled watching each gymnast do ten sky-high jumps. Gymnasts do flips, twists, and somersaults during each jump. Judges score these gymnasts on how hard the moves are and how high they jump.

Japanese gymnast Yasuhiro Ueyama does a back flip on the trampoline.

Rio2016

Cheer Them On!

Gymnasts do amazing moves. They flip. They spin and twirl. They jump high into the air. It's no wonder people love to watch these thrilling events. Get ready for the Summer Games. Sit back and cheer for your favorite athletes!

You Hao of China earned a bronze medal for his pommel horse routine.

Glossary

all-around event A competition in which gymnasts perform on all the apparatuses.

apparatus A piece of equipment on which gymnasts do routines.

difficulty points In artistic gymnastics, the point value of for each move; harder moves have higher point values.

execution points In artistic gymnastics, the points given for how well a gymnast does moves; a gymnast starts with 10 execution points and points are taken away for mistakes.

prop An object or element used in rhythmic gymnastics; clubs, hoops, ribbons, and balls are used in the Olympics.

qualifying round The round to determine who will be in the final competition.